101 Top Secret
Public Speaking Strategies

*Speak with Confidence
Get Success!*

Andy O'Sullivan

Beatrice

To whom I owe it all

LEGAL NOTICES

The information presented herein represents the view of the author as of the date of publication. Because of the rate with which conditions change, the author's reserve the right to alter and update his opinion based on the new conditions. This book is for informational purposes only. While every attempt has been made to verify the information provided in this book, neither the authors nor their affiliates/partners assume any responsibility for errors, inaccuracies or omissions. Any slights of people or organizations are unintentional. If advice concerning legal, financial or any other real estate related matters is needed, the services of a fully qualified professional should be sought. This book is not intended for use as a source of legal or accounting advice.

STATEMENT OF EARNINGS/DISCLAIMER. Every effort has been made to accurately represent this product and its potential. Examples in these materials are not to be interpreted as a promise or guarantee of earnings. Earning potential is entirely dependent on the person using our product, ideas and techniques. We do not purport this as a "get rich scheme."

Your level of success in attaining the results claimed in our materials depends on the time you devote to the program, ideas and techniques mentioned, your finances, knowledge and various skills. Since these factors differ according to individuals, we cannot guarantee your success or income level. Nor are we responsible for any of your actions.

Materials in our product and our website may contain information that includes or is based upon forward-looking statements. Forward-looking statements give our expectations or forecasts of future events. You can identify these statements by the fact that they do not relate strictly to historical or current facts. They use words such as "anticipate," "estimate," "expect," "project," "intend," "plan," "believe," and other words and terms of similar meaning in connection with a description of potential earnings or financial performance.

ALL RIGHTS RESERVED. No part of this book may be reproduced or transmitted in any form whatsoever, electronic, or mechanical, including photocopying, recording, or by any informational storage or retrieval without the expressed written consent of the authors.

© Andy O'Sullivan

If you do not wish to be bound by the above, you may return this book to the publisher for a full refund.

TABLE OF CONTENTS

Introduction	Who is Andy O'Sullivan	13
	Why You Will Want to Listen	
	How He Will Save You Pain	
CHAPTER 1	**Fear of Speaking in Public**	**33**
1	Feel Anxious or Stressed?	34
2	Perfect Presentations	36
3	Accepting Anxiety	37
4	Persecuted in a Presentation	39
5	Seeking Support	40
6	Assistance and Encouragement	41
7	Breathing Fears and Anxiety Away	42
CHAPTER 2	**Researching and Preparing a Presentation**	**45**
8	Expertise or Ego	46
9	Making the Subject Interesting	47
10	Chat to Colleagues	48
11	Essential Preparation	49
12	Make it Relevant	50

CHAPTER 3 Presentation Planning — 51
- 13 Reviewing for Ideas — 52
- 14 Confirming the Objective — 53
- 15 Persuading the Meeting — 54
- 16 Helping with Understanding — 55
- 17 Ensure They Have Fun — 56
- 18 Keeping the Lid on It — 57
- 19 For, Against or Indifferent — 58
- 20 Seeking Their Thoughts — 59

CHAPTER 4 Content Creation — 61
- 21 Slowing the Race — 62
- 22 Rejecting the Rules — 64
- 23 Being Understood — 66
- 24 See the Scene — 67
- 25 Losing an I — 69
- 26 Share a Story — 70
- 27 One and Only — 71
- 28 Being Open to Emotions — 73
- 29 Seeing the Benefits — 74
- 30 Uncovering Humour — 75
- 31 Hands Up! — 77
- 32 Taking the Lead — 79
- 33 Limit the Details — 80
- 34 Indirect Persuasion — 81
- 35 Defining the Details — 83
- 36 Finishing on a Positive — 85

Contents

CHAPTER 5	Rehearse & Review	**87**
37	Starting Early	88
38	Focussed Improvement	89
39	Important Part of Preparation	91
40	Feeding on Feedback	93
41	Seeing the Slides	94
42	Review and Customise	95
43	Winning Modifications	96
44	Raising Your Profile	97
45	Selecting Keywords	99
46	Shortening Their Path	100
47	Adding a Blank	102
48	Staying Silent	103
CHAPTER 6	**Helping with Handouts**	**105**
49	Passing the Handout	106
50	Separating Your Handouts	108
51	Spacing Your Points	109
52	Figuring the Information	110
53	Colouring Your Content	111
54	Following Up	113
55	Paper Can Be Best	114
56	Writing to Be Seen	116

CHAPTER 7	Stepping into The Speaking Area	117
57	Walking as a Reader	118
58	Stop and Stand	121
59	Returning to the Start	122
CHAPTER 8	Confidently Answering Questions	123
60	Timing Your Session	124
61	Check In With Colleagues	125
62	Repeat in Reply	126
63	Pause, Then Speak	127
64	Validate the Question	128
65	Staying on Course	130
66	Ask a Colleague	131
67	Terminating the Session	132
CHAPTER 9	Using Your Voice and Body for Intent and Influence	133
68	Slowing the Speed	134
69	Speeding Up	135
70	Authentic Connection	136
71	Looking to Include Everyone	137
72	Helping Hands	138
73	Sending Signals and Signs	139
74	What Looks Will Reveal	142

CHAPTER 10	Recording and Reviewing	**143**
75	Filming Assistance	144
76	Repetitive and Redundant	145
77	Showing Significance	146

CHAPTER 11	Planning for Success	**147**
78	Planning Your Preparations	148
79	Contingency Planning	149
80	Affirming Access	150
81	An Outfit to Fit In	151
82	Lubricating a Symptom of Stress	152
83	Taking the Time	154

CHAPTER 12	Arriving in the Room	**157**
84	Clearing the Way	158
85	Clearly Heard	159
86	Can You Hear Me?	160
87	Sensing the Space	161
88	High Lighting Your Speech	162
89	Sprucing up the Suit	163
90	Stand and Stretch	164
91	Settling into Your Speech	165

CHAPTER 12	Arriving in the Room *Continued*	157
92	Walking Straight	166
93	Slanted Stance	167
94	Who's Listening?	168
95	Sensible Suggestions	169
96	Speaking Out Against	171
97	Focus on Serving	172
98	Slow and Steady	174
99	Seeking Support Seeing the Laughter	175
100	Peak	176
101	Question Yourself	177

About Andy O'Sullivan   **181**

Acknowledgements   **185**

References   **189**

Bibliography   **191**

INTRODUCTION

Who is Andy O'Sullivan... and How You Can Now Benefit From All His Pain, Panic and Practice

You may have noticed that whenever there are young children around, they are always happy to play and perform in public.

They are happy to dance, sing, or play instruments in front of family, friends and neighbours.

They will happily do all these things without any fears or worries about getting embarrassed, looking silly or even being judged.

Then something happens to change us.

Something happens that causes us to change the way we see ourselves. This change now makes us worry about what others will think about us.

This change occurs somewhere between childhood and adulthood. It is a change that steals away all the natural confidence we all had when we were born and enjoyed throughout those early years of life.

Rather than feeling happy, relaxed and even excited to perform in front of others, grabbing every opportunity we could ever find, we are now fearful when standing and speaking.

These feelings of fear, panic and pending doom take over immediately we are faced with the ordeal of having to speak in public.

Just the thought of standing and speaking at a meeting that may be weeks away is enough to fill our bodies with all those feelings of dread and fear.

Introduction

If the idea of speaking in public now fills us with all these unpleasant feelings, I am sure having to sing or dance in front of other people would for many now be a whole lot worse!

What Changed?

So what has happened to change things for us?

What is it that has changed us from feeling happy and confident when performing to now having all those negative feelings fill our bodies whenever we are in these situations?

You may have heard of the 'fight or flight response' we have whenever we are placed in a stressful situation, like delivering a pitch.

While this is likely to have played a part in my fear of public speaking, there was another factor that affected how I felt about standing in front of large groups with everyone looking at me.

A big part of my fear and, dare I even say, hatred of speaking in public was all down to my early education.

As I now look back, it is a pity that neither of the schools that I attended ever had a programme where they would help us to develop our communication skills and confidence.

These are the skills so critical to achieving success throughout our professional lives.

If anything, the way the schools operated was totally the opposite.

Punishment and Embarrassment

At my schools, public speaking was used as a punishment by many of my teachers.

If the teachers felt you or the class were misbehaving in any way, they would force us to read either our work or, even worse, from a textbook to the whole class.

Introduction

As a young child, struggling to read in front of the class of thirty or so other children, I would naturally stumble or hesitate over some of the words.

This situation was more likely to occur if the words were new to me or in another language that I was learning at the time.

What was the result?

The whole class would immediately erupt into laughter, sometimes even pointing and making unpleasant comments.

I would be left standing there in front of the entire class feeling embarrassed, upset and very much alone.

Placing a child in this position was not a way to help build their confidence and self-esteem during those early formative years.

It was not the fault of all the other children in my class in the way they behaved towards me.

Nor was it mine when I did the same during their public reading sessions as they too stumbled over their words, sometimes silently standing there, red with embarrassment.

Haunting Memories

Throughout my school days, speaking or reading in public therefore became an experience to be feared and one to avoid at all costs.

When I meet up with some of my old school friends, we are still haunted by the experiences of those public reading punishments, decades later.

Does this make my fear of public speaking the fault of my teachers?

Introduction

They were the ones who made the idea of speaking in public something to be feared, making us individually stand up in front of the whole class and read to everyone.

I used to think it was.

Reflecting to Forgive

Now, on reflection, I feel they would never genuinely do anything if they knew the effect it would have on us.

Little did they know the effect these regular humiliations would have on both my classmates and me as we grew up and became adults.

In many of the private schools here in the UK and other education systems around the world, they actively encourage and support public speaking.

Schools will have debating clubs and inter-school contests all aimed at developing their students' speaking skills.

Training in how to communicate and confidently speak in public is something I would love to see in every school, worldwide.

Adulthood

As a young adult, I would always hate being the centre of attention and therefore would work to ensure it was avoided at all costs.

This hatred had an immense effect on both my career and even whenever I was out socialising.

Many years ago, after starting a trainee job at a new company, I was always invited out for some after work drinks on Fridays.

In the bar with my new colleagues, we would often have other people from the department in which we worked join us.

These were people who I had never met or had only had a very brief conversation with.

Introduction

Vividly I recall how the thought of having to stand there in front of everyone, with them all looking at me, totally scared me as I asked the straightforward question of what drink they would like.

Standing in front of the group, with them all staring at me, was public speaking and I hated it!

It was something that I wanted to avoid at all costs, so came up with an ingenious plan.

Whenever it came to buying a round of drinks (which I was delighted to do), I would always ask one of my close colleagues to get the drinks in and I would give them the money.

Easy!

On reflection, as I was never seen to buy any drinks, all the other people who joined us for those Friday drinks probably perceived me as being very tight with money.

My colleagues, on the other hand, must have been seen to be very generous.

Either way, getting my colleagues to take the orders and buy the drinks never helped me to overcome my fear of speaking in public.

Avoidance

Throughout my career, I carried on taking every opportunity possible to avoid being in the same situation of speaking in public.

This avoidance would often mean not participating in meetings where there were many attendees or feeling unable to voice my opinion to any proposals presented, even when I was against them.

Introduction

Career Block

The lack of confidence to speak in public would affect my career as changing jobs and attending the inevitable interviews were all part of the process.

It would entail having to sit in the interview with people asking lots of questions while looking at me.

This was scary!

If an interview with one or two people scared me, the idea of a panel type process was entirely out of the question.

The thought of facing an interview panel scared me so much, I would avoid applying for any jobs where this was a known part of the process.

While trying to secure what I felt would be my ideal job, there could be other unexpected hurdles.

Once, having cruised through the interview process for what I felt was the perfect job, I hit a huge hurdle.

The company decided all of the shortlisted candidates would need to deliver a 3 to 5 minute presentation to the members of the department in which they would work if successful in their application.

I could not think of anything worse and immediately withdrew my application for the role.

Facing one or two people in an interview was a terrifying thought for me. The idea of a public presentation was just too much.

Achieving My Potential

It was some years later while working for an international bank that my fears of speaking up in public came to a head.

Introduction

My management always perceived me to be a 'good worker', which I was, but something was missing. I wanted more.

Being ambitious, I naturally wanted to have more success in my career, to get promoted, to have a more substantial salary.

Continually, I kept seeing newer and less experienced colleagues climbing the corporate career ladder ahead of me.

What was it that they were doing to get this success?

Speaking and Saying Nothing New

These colleagues were the ones who were always actively participating in meetings.

You would find that they would always have an opinion to share in meetings, especially when senior management were present.

On most occasions, the views and ideas they shared were not even their own!

Sometimes all they would do is just repeat and rephrase what somebody else in the meeting had already stated.

Continually, these were the same people the management liked.

While I stayed in exactly the same role, never moving up the corporate career ladder, my colleagues who spoke up became the people who always got noticed, promoted and rewarded.

It became abundantly clear to me that, no matter how hard you work, no matter what hours you are putting in, working evenings and weekends, to stand any chance of getting success, you have to be seen and heard.

That is when it dawned on me! I had to improve my communication skills.

Introduction

The Journey

As I started out on what was for me a long and tough journey to becoming a more confident public speaker and presenter, I was continually on the lookout for that 'magic pill'.

The one simple step or strategy that would quickly allow me always to feel confident whenever I needed to speak in public.

In my search for this 'magic pill', I started attending countless courses, workshops and seminars and reading all the books on public speaking that I could find.

There were also all of the online courses, articles and videos which I spent many, many hours devouring over my evenings and weekends.

You can find countless tips, tools and techniques on the internet.

They all seem to promise they will help us become better speakers, to have more confidence, to deal better with all those surprise speaking situations.

To the uninitiated, there is also a lot of, dare I say, 'rubbish' that is said about public speaking.

At best it is worthless, while at the worst, it will damage your confidence and along with it any chance you have of achieving success.

After wasting much time and money being given a false belief of instant confidence, having been taught techniques that are ridiculous, I came to what is an obvious conclusion.

There is no 'magic pill'.

Not one simple technique will give you the confidence and skills to allow you to deal with an awkward question, argumentative client or cope when things go terribly wrong.

Introduction

It was after this realisation that I began what was to become a long and, at times, painful journey of growth.

A journey that would take me from being filled with panic, days before I was due to deliver a pitch or presentation.

Where I would spend days rehearsing my every word, only to deliver pitches and presentations that were seen as a 'major embarrassment'.
Not my words.

Those were the words of my manager at the time.

The very person that I had always been hoping to impress by speaking in public.

Not A Natural

You can probably guess, even as an adult, I was not a 'natural' public speaker, yet today that is precisely what everyone perceives me as being.

When people see me regularly delivering perfect pitches or presentations in large auditoriums, they tell me afterwards that I am a 'natural' and how easy it is for 'people like me'.

Those who see me delivering confident speeches and presentations, even off-the-cuff, have not witnessed or seen the pain and panic that got me into the position where I am today, regularly winning awards and recognition for all my continual achievements.

The journey I have been through over all these years was not pleasant or enjoyable, yet it has taught me a tremendous amount.

It has taught me what works, and most importantly what does not.

It is all this first-hand knowledge and experience that is now available for you in this book.

Lucky you!

Introduction

You now get the benefit of all the pain, stress and upset that I went through, which will now ensure you become confident and competent as you now successfully create and deliver winning speeches, presentations and pitches with the tips in this book.

Enjoy the journey….

I will be here every step of the way.

Andy O'Sullivan
andy@academyofpublicspeakers.com
www.academyofpublicspeakers.com
Books: - http://andy.chat/books
LinkedIn: - http://andy.chat/linkedin
Twitter: - http://andy.chat/twitter
Facebook: - http://andy.chat/facebook

Public Speaking Strategies

Chapter 1

Fear of Speaking in Public

1

Feel Anxious or Stressed?

When thinking about your upcoming presentation, do you feel uncomfortable?

Perhaps it makes you feel a bit stressed?

Maybe anxious?

Perhaps you think it is better to leave the preparation for another day?

Continued

1

Feel Anxious or Stressed?

Continued

This is the approach that I used when first delivering presentations, but it only made the anxiety worse as the meeting date approached.

When you start preparing your presentation ahead of time, it will give you plenty of time for rehearsals and fine-tuning, reducing any anxiety and building your confidence.

2

Perfect Presentations

A common cause of public speaking anxiety amongst my clients is wanting to deliver a speech that is impeccable, with every word and action being rehearsed to precise perfection.

Seeking this level of perfection is common, yet unrealistic and even undesirable.

People will be attending the meeting for a presentation rather than to see a perfect, polished performance.

Prepare and practice to the level you feel you are able to deliver an authentic, professional presentation.

3

Accepting Anxiety

One step to help you with any anxiety is to acknowledge that you may make a mistake when presenting at the meeting.

That's ok!

You will have seen other speakers making mistakes in the past without giving it a second thought.

It is unlikely anyone attending will notice any mistake that you happen to make, and if they do, it will soon be forgotten.

Continued

3

Accepting Anxiety

Continued

Acknowledging and accepting little mistakes can occasionally happen while you are speaking, will free you from the worry that they could occur.

This acknowledgement will now help to reduce any public speaking anxiety, helping you feel more relaxed and confident.

4

Persecuted in a Presentation

Pre-meeting anxiety may have you imagining everyone attending has spent days secretly hatching plans to ask you lots of awkward or tricky questions.

Most attendees probably will not even have thought about the meeting or your speech until a few moments before leaving their desks.

Let go of these concerns, maintaining focus on how you can help everyone attending with the content of your presentation.

5

Seeking Support

First delivering your presentation to a small, supportive group of colleagues or friends will help to build your confidence.

The opportunity to rehearse in front of them, along with their support, encouragement and feedback will ensure you feel more confident for the meeting at which you have been asked to deliver the presentation.

6

Assistance and Encouragement

Chewing a piece of gum in the lead up to your presentation may help you to feel more relaxed as it can lower levels of hormones associated with stress according to a study by scientists at Tokushima University (Mail Online 2018).

While the gum may help you to relax, remember to discreetly remove and dispose of it before walking to the front of the room to start your presentation.

7

Breathing Fears and Anxiety Away

When you are in the meeting room and feeling anxious, there can be a tendency to take fast, shallow breaths.

This type of breathing increases the stress levels in those key moments when we what to feel calm and in control.

Follow this '4 Square' breathing technique to steady your nerves, while regulating your breathing rate, so you will begin to feel more relaxed.

Continued

7

Breathing Fears and Anxiety Away

Continued

Place both feet flat on the floor and relax your arms to the side.

>Slowly and quietly breathe in for 4 seconds.
>
>Hold your breath for 4 seconds.
>
>Slowly breathe out for 4 seconds.
>
>Hold for 4 seconds.
>
>Breathe in for 4 seconds.

Continued

7

Breathing Fears and Anxiety Away

Continued

As you repeat this cycle of slow and regulated breathing, you will feel your body relaxing and all the stress slowly slipping away.

The 4 Square breathing technique can be used in any situations where you feel anxious and while standing or sitting without anyone knowing or noticing what you are doing.

Chapter 2

Researching and Preparing a Presentation

8

Expertise or Ego

When you are invited to deliver a presentation at a meeting, consider if it is a subject that you have the appropriate knowledge and experience to speak on.

If you feel otherwise, the person inviting you will be grateful if you are able to suggest a suitable colleague who has the expertise suited for the occasion or purpose of the meeting.

9

Making the Subject Interesting

Ask your manager or the person who invited you to speak at the meeting if there are any particular points or areas that they would like you to cover in your presentation.

Covering these points will ingratiate you with your manager and the audience.

In the meeting, they will see your presentation as having been created just for them, even if it has been adapted from one used previously.

10

Chat to Colleagues

If you are presenting at your team meeting, this is one task to complete before creating your presentation.

Take the time to chat with colleagues to see what they would like you to cover and any questions they may already have on your subject.

You will then be able to include their questions in your presentation content and feel far better prepared for any others that arise.

11

Essential Preparation

Well before the meeting starts at which you are speaking, you will need to prepare yourself mentally for delivering the presentation.

Knowing how many people are expected to be attending the meeting is an essential part of your preparation.

Speaking in front of 4 people will require different mental preparation to when 40 are attending the meeting.

12

Make it Relevant

People will naturally pay more attention to speakers who are covering topics in the meeting that are relevant to their: -

    Career

    Role

    Salary

    Interests

When you find out what is important to your audience, you are able to make your speech relevant to them so that everyone will pay attention to you.

Chapter 3

Presentation Planning

13

Reviewing for Ideas

As you are structuring your speech, take time to regularly review the notes made of your thoughts, ideas, concepts or feelings.

Reviewing your notes can in turn trigger other ideas that may be useful and worth including in your presentation.

14

Confirming the Objective

The primary objective of the speech is something you will want to decide on before you start to create it.

Would your objective in the meeting be to: -

    Inform

    Persuade

    Entertain

There can be a crossover between these speech types which we will cover in the following pages.

15

Persuading the Meeting

A persuasive speech will be one in which the speaker is aiming to convince an audience to accept their point of view on a proposal, product or idea.

You might create a persuasive speech when: -

> Convincing a team of your plan.
>
> Pitching a business idea.
>
> Presenting your experience when attending an interview.
>
> Selling a concept or idea.

16

Helping with Understanding

Informative speeches have the key purpose of relaying information, knowledge, or experience to the meeting attendees that will enhance their understanding.

Examples of where this type of speech would be presented are when explaining: -

>How to use a new system.
>
>A new approach to increasing sales.
>
>The impact of a team reorganisation.

17

Ensure They Have Fun

An entertaining speech is delivered with the purpose of helping the audience to enjoy the occasion as they relax, maybe laugh, but certainly have fun at the event.

A well-known example of where you will hear an entertaining speech is from the Best Man at a wedding.

The aim is to use stories and anecdotes to entertain the audience.

18

Keeping the Lid on It

Structuring your speech is the first step for you to take.

Opening your laptop and starting PowerPoint is the stage that should only come after you have created your speech.

An effective presentation has the slides used to support your speech, rather than having the speech support the slides.

19

For, Against or Indifferent

What do the people attending the meeting to hear your speech think about the subject?

Will any of them have any preconceptions or hold views for or against the subject of your speech?

This will be useful information for you to find out.

Knowing this information in advance is crucial as it will help you to prepare a presentation that addresses their preconceptions or views.

20

Seeking Their Thoughts

If you are presenting a proposal that you know will have some opposition, ask questions early on in your presentation.

Asking questions to the meeting attendees will draw out their concerns, thoughts and opinions on your proposal.

It is more persuasive and effective for you to deal with any opposition to the proposal in the early stages of your presentation.

Public Speaking Strategies

Chapter 4

Content Creation

21

Slowing the Race

A temptation for new speakers is to cram absolutely everything they know about a subject into their speech.

They feel all their knowledge and experience needs to be shared to help the audience grasp the subject to the same level as theirs.

Continued

21

Slowing the Race

Continued

The speaker then has to race through all the content to get it covered in time, leaving their audience dazed and overwhelmed.

It is far better for the audience if you only include the facts and information required to convey the core idea of your speech.

22

Rejecting the Rules

As the speech is not going to be graded by your English teacher, there is no need to worry about creating it using impeccable English grammar.

Each of the short sentences you write/type out for your speech will only need to have the words required for you to understand the point being made.

Omitting words will help to make the speech easier to learn and recall.

Continued

22

Rejecting the Rules

Continued

For example, the sentence 'to quickly summarise what it is we have covered in this presentation today' becomes 'to summarise what we have covered'.

While delivering the speech, you can add in or swap words as the aim is to be a natural speaker rather than word perfect.

23

Being Understood

We each have our own favourite metaphors that we use without a thought in our day-to-day conversations.

For example, we may describe a person as being as 'cool as a cucumber' as they 'hit the home run'.

When creating a presentation for an audience with diverse interests and backgrounds, eliminate any phrases, words or sayings that may not be understood by every person in the audience.

24

See the Scene

Sensory words are more powerful and memorable than many of the more familiar words we usually use in our everyday speech.

Examples of our everyday words are: -

    Feel
    Hear
    See
    Smell
    Taste

Continued

24

See the Scene

Continued

Examples of sensory words are: -

> Sticky
> Hum
> Round
> Musty
> Spicy

To help your audience with their recall, see how you can incorporate sensory words into your next speech.

25

Losing an I

Seek to avoid starting your speech with those "I" focused sentences you will often hear all the other speakers using.

Examples are: -

> "I'm here today…'
>
> "I'm going to tell you…"
>
> "I want to…"

The opening of your speech will have more impact when it is about your audience rather than you.

26

Share a Story

To help your audience understand the point you are making in your speech, include specific examples.

If the stories used come from clients or colleagues, everyone will find it easier to relate to them.

For example, rather than saying 'we need to provide a higher level of customer service', share a story of when a colleague did just that and the impact it had.

27

One and Only

There is one unique difference between you and every other person speaking at the same meeting.

In fact, it is the same difference that separates you from everyone else in the world.

It is each and every one of your personal life experiences.

These may be from home, school, work or any other challenges that you have faced.

Continued

27

One and Only

Continued

What personal life experiences do you have that you would feel comfortable sharing with those attending the meeting?

Sharing experiences that fit the message of your speech can help bring it to life and leave a long-lasting impression on your audience.

28

Being Open to Emotions

When you are sharing stories in your speech, see how you can connect people with the feelings felt at the time.

Share and connect them with your emotions, thoughts, worries or concerns.

This will bring the whole story to life.

Rather than retelling it, relive it.

29

Seeing the Benefits

When your presentation is covering an issue with a proposed solution, help meeting attendees to appreciate the problem, its cause, and potential outcome if left, by covering these areas first in your presentation.

Once people have an appreciation and understanding of the issue, it will be time to move on to your proposed solution.

Following the structure of problem - cause - solution will help attendees to see the benefits of your proposal.

30

Uncovering Humour

Humour is a wonderful way of creating a connection and deepening the engagement with your audience.

While you may feel that you are not that funny, it can be tempting to find jokes on the internet that can easily be included into each of the presentations you create and deliver.

The internet is one place best avoided for this to work successfully for you.

Continued

30

Uncovering Humour

Continued

It is best to leave all those jokes found on the internet for when you are in social situations.

Rather than adding any forced humour or artificial jokes to your speech, take the time to discover and develop the inherent humour already in the stories you have included.

31

Hands Up!

As a way of getting everyone attending a meeting involved and engaged, speakers will often ask a question that requires attendees to raise their hand.

The single question they ask will only see one part of the audience raising their hands and participating.

Consider how you can structure the question to ensure everyone will participate by having an opportunity to raise their hand.

Continued

31

Hands Up!

Continued

To achieve this, you are likely to need additional follow-up questions.

This example of questions would ensure that everyone attending raises their hand at some point: -

    Who drinks tea?

    Who drinks coffee?

    Who drinks neither?

32

Taking the Lead

When requesting a show of hands, lead the way by putting your hand up.

Start raising your hand when you are a couple of words from the end of your question.

Taking the lead makes it easier for everyone to process the information and know the action they are expected to take.

Raising your hand will result in higher involvement from those attending the meeting.

33

Limit the Details

The purpose of a presentation is for you to share information with everyone attending the meeting.

Resist the urge to use it as an opportunity to show off how much you know on the subject to your clients, colleagues or boss.

Include just enough data, evidence or information to help them understand your points and the topic you are covering.

34

Indirect Persuasion

Are you aiming to convince or persuade those attending the meeting at which you are speaking to adopt your point of view or proposal?

When delivering a presentation that is persuasive in purpose, seek to replace words that are direct.

Examples of direct words are: -

    Could
    Should
    Must

Continued

Public Speaking Strategies

34

Indirect Persuasion

Continued

It will help to keep everyone's mind open to your proposal and more likely to accept it when you replace them with indirect words such as: -

    Maybe

    Might

    Perhaps

35

Defining the Details

When presenting to people who are already aware of your subject, it is advisable to limit the amount of information covered in the opening minutes as you set the scene.

For example, when speaking about a new system that is going to be installed in the organisation, at the first meeting you may give attendees the background and rationale for the decision.

Continued

35

Defining the Details

Continued

Subsequent meetings with the same attendees will only need to recap this information briefly.

When a speaker repeats the same information to an equal level of detail at every meeting, people will feel it is a waste of their time and start to deliberately arrive late, assuming they know what will be covered in the first part of the meeting.

36

Finishing on a Positive

There are occasions when the subject of your speech will have created ardent debate or sharing of views in the meeting.

If you have been speaking on a contentious or controversial subject, aim to close your speech on an inspiring and positive note.

With a speech closing that is inspiring and positive, your audience will feel more encouraged and open to adopting the idea proposed as they reflect on what you have presented to them.

Public Speaking Strategies

Chapter 5

Review and Rehearse

37

Starting Early

The nerves and fear of public speaking can cause you to procrastinate about starting to prepare your presentation.

When you take the opportunity to complete your notes and any required slides, you will have far more time for the rehearsals.

Preparing your presentation may seem like something to put off, but you will be glad you started and prepared early when it is time to present at the meeting!

Review and Rehearse

38

Focussed Improvement

When first rehearsing your speech, you will find it easier to focus on improving one area before moving on to the next.

For example, you could individually focus on improving the: -

      1. Words

      2. Pace

      3. Gestures

      4. Staging

Continued

38

Focussed Improvement

Continued

As you rehearse your speech focussed on improving one area to your satisfaction before moving on to the next, you will quickly start to see the progress that will now build your confidence.

These areas of public speaking skills are covered in more detail in the following tips.

39

Important Part of Preparation

While rehearsing your speech, you are likely to fine-tune the content that you have previously created.

This may include: -

- Substituting sections of your speech.
- Swapping the order covered.
- Replacing individual words and phrases.

Continued

39

Important Part of Preparation

Continued

To save yourself from feeling rushed and under pressure, allow yourself adequate time for this important part of your preparation.

As we covered in the previous tip, your confidence will grow as you see improvements in your speech and feel comfortable with the content you are going to share in the meeting.

40

Feeding on Feedback

Take the opportunity to rehearse all your presentations in front of family, friends or supportive colleagues.

Ask them to give you feedback on how you can improve and be even better.

Check to see if they understood the fundamental purpose of your presentation and the action you wanted them to take.

If it is not clear to them, it is unlikely to be clear to your audience.

41

Seeing the Slides

Speakers will sometimes have a look of surprise when a slide appears on the screen during their presentation.

A bewildered look appears on their face as though it is the first time they have ever seen the slide.

Rehearse with your slide presentation, so you get to know the order and purpose of each one that you have included.

42

Review and Customise

There are times when you will be invited to deliver a presentation that you have previously given at another meeting.

As this will be a different audience, take the time to review and customise each of your slides as well as your content as required for this session.

Making any required customisations to the presentation for this new audience will help to ensure its suitability for their needs and that it fulfils your objectives.

43

Winning Modifications

Everyone attending the meeting, including those sitting at the back, will want to be able to read all the text on the slides.

Take a moment to see if all the slides can be read before anyone arrives in the room, so you are able to make any adjustments that are required.

For example, you may find it will help to: -

    Increase the size of the font
    Change to a different typeface
    Use a different coloured font

44

Raising Your Profile

Speaking in a meeting is a wonderful opportunity to raise your profile within the department and organisation.

To help do this positively, only include artwork and pictures in your slides that have either been purchased or for which you have a licence.

If there is a copyright message written across the artwork on a slide, it will be evident to everyone attending the meeting that the image has not been purchased.

Continued

44

Raising Your Profile

Continued

Using unlicensed artwork will have the meeting attendees questioning both your credibility and honesty.

Something you will want to avoid when trying to: -

>Get that new job
>Impress the boss
>Win business
>Secure an investment

45

Selecting Keywords

When attending a presentation, one of the clear giveaways that the speaker has not adequately prepared for their presentation is when the slides consist of long sentences and paragraphs.

The lines of text will have been added for the speaker's benefit as they need to use it for their script.

When creating your presentation, rather than having line after line of text, aim to have just a few keywords or an image on the slide to help your audience with their understanding of the point you are sharing with them.

46

Shortening Their Path

When the location of the resources you include in your presentation are on external sites with a long address, you will find it will be easier for people to type them out correctly if a URL shortening service is used.

URL shortening can be achieved with many of the free and premium services like: -

    bit.ly
    goo.gl
    tinyurl.com

Continued

46

Shortening Their Path

Continued

When a website address has been shortened with one of these services, you will be able to share the URL like this: -

> https://is.gd/go_here

Rather than: -

> https://www.academyofpublicspeakers.com/corporate-confidence-live-training

47

Adding a Blank

Has your side presentation been finalised?

Once your presentation has been created and finalised, add an extra blank slide or two at the end.

As you reach the end of your presentation, if you happen to click once too often accidentally, the blank slides will display rather than ending the show and showing your desktop.

48

Staying Silent

If your presentation slide has an image or any content that is going to have an impact on the attendees, remain silent slightly longer as the slide displays on the screen.

The impact a slide may have on the attendees can be when showing: -

    A quote

    Financial Data

    Detailed statistics

    A compelling picture

Continued

48

Staying Silent

Continued

By staying silent, you will provide the audience with the additional time they require to take in the information displayed.

If you continue speaking at this point, the audience is likely to miss out on some of what you say, as their attention will still be on the slide and the impact it had on them.

Chapter 6

Helping with Handouts

49

Passing the Handout

If you are providing handouts to the meeting audience to help with their understanding of your presentation, consider in advance the best time for them to be distributed.

When the handouts are passed around the room and read by the audience, they will become the focus of everyone's attention.

Continued

49

Passing the Handout

Continued

While the documents are being passed around, if you continue speaking, the meeting audience will miss out on what you are saying as they read the documents.

It may be better for you to either distribute the handouts at the beginning or end of the meeting to remove the distraction and to help the audience focus on you and your presentation.

50

Separating Your Handouts

Create any handouts you plan to use separately from your presentation slides.

The information they contain and the purpose of each are entirely different.

A handout is taken away from the presentation and used as a reference to the information that you shared with the meeting audience.

Slides are used solely as an aid to your presentation, containing only key points and graphics.

51

Spacing Your Points

When the handouts are organised to follow the same structure as your presentation, they will be easier for your audience to use.

Including extra space around your images, graphs and text will provide an area for your audience to write in their own notes and any questions for the later Q&A session.

52

Figuring the Information

While delivering your presentation, it will help the audience if they are able to follow along in the handouts you have provided.

When creating handouts, include the page numbers at the bottom of each sheet.

As you move through the presentation, you will be able to help the meeting audience by referring to information on specific pages of the handout.

53

Colouring Your Content

Aim to have your handouts printed on coloured paper, as doing so will serve several purposes.

As the attendees view your handout, the coloured paper will prove to be visually more interesting to them than ordinary plain white paper.

If there are other people presenting at the same meeting, both you and your coloured handouts will stand out as being different and distinct.

Continued

53

Colouring Your Content

Continued

Having your handouts printed on coloured paper will help to serve another purpose long after the meeting has finished.

When the meeting attendees gather up their papers and return to their desks, your coloured handouts will be conspicuous amongst all their other documents, making them more likely to be referenced in the future.

54

Following Up

After your presentation and the meeting are over, help the attendees to contact you with any follow up questions.

You can do this by including on your handouts details such as your name, email address and phone number.

Including your contact details on the handouts allows attendees to see who they can contact for further information weeks, months or maybe even years later when they review the information you provided.

55

Paper Can Be Best

How do you illustrate the points of your presentations?

It is likely that you will use an application like one of these: -

> PowerPoint
> Keynote
> Prezi

With all the amazing features available to us in these and similar applications, it is so easy to neglect the traditional flip chart.

Continued

55

Paper Can Be Best

Continued

The flip chart can be used to quickly capture and record attendee's comments, thoughts and ideas.

This is especially useful when used in small meetings and events.

56

Writing to Be Seen

When writing on a flip chart or whiteboard, will everyone attending the meeting be able to see what you have written?

It will be easier for your audience if you use a dark coloured pen to write in block capital letters that are large enough for those sitting at the back to easily read.

Select a different colour ink to underline or circle text that is important so that it stands out.

Chapter

7

Stepping into The Speaking Area

57

Walking as a Reader

In English, we read the sentences in all of our books, newspapers and magazines from left to right.

This same left to right movement can be used to help the meeting attendees with their understanding by creating a timeline of the situation or events we are sharing.

Continued

57

Walking as a Reader

Continued

As you start speaking about what occurred in the past, make your way over to your right which is the audience's left.

Remain in this area to deliver this part of your speech.

When it then comes to discussing where we are now and the current situation, slowly walk over to the centre of the speaking area.

Continued

57

Walking as a Reader

Continued

Finally, as it now comes to talking about what can be achieved in the future, walk to your left which is your audience's right.

This three-stage structure will help with the audience's awareness and appreciation of the situation you are sharing with them.

58

Stop and Stand

When approaching a key point in your presentation, audience attention can be drawn to it with your movement within the speaking area.

When leading up to the key point that you are about to make and walking within the speaking area, turn to fully face the audience, pause, and then deliver your point.

Standing still removes all other distractions, allowing the audience to be entirely focused on your words rather than your movements.

59

Returning to the Start

As you start to reach the end of your presentation, make your way back to the same central spot you originally stood when starting.

Staying at this spot as you deliver your closing sentences will help to make your presentation more homogeneous and memorable.

Chapter 8

Confidently Answering Questions

60

Timing Your Session

When planning your presentation Q&A session, consider how long you will need to allocate for this part of the meeting.

If you are presenting on a complicated or controversial subject with a large number of people attending the meeting, it is likely more time will be required for questions than if you were speaking on a routine matter to a couple of colleagues.

Allocating enough time for the Q&A session will ensure you are able to address any concerns or questions that are in the minds of your audience.

61

Check In With Colleagues

It can be more challenging for colleagues or clients to participate in your Q&A session when they are joining the meeting from a remote location.

Take a moment to check in with them to see if they have any questions on what you have covered.

They will feel valued and appreciate you taking the time to ask.

62

Repeat in Reply

You will notice in larger meetings that people sitting close to the front will usually speak quieter than those sitting towards the back when asking questions.

To help ensure everyone in the room has heard the question, you may need to repeat it before starting your answer.

Repeating the question will ensure everyone can then understand the context of the points you are making in reply.

63

Pause, Then Speak

In the Q&A sessions of many presentations, I have often seen speakers asking for every one of the questions to be repeated.

After a while, the audience starts to see this as a way to delay answering the question.

If you have genuinely not heard, do ask for the question to be repeated before starting to answer.

When you have heard the question, pause for a second and then start to deliver your reply.

64

Validate the Question

As other speakers answer audience questions, they can often be heard starting their answer with a phrase similar to 'that is a good question'.

If this phrase is repeatedly used as their standard first sentence, it has little value, even if the person was asking a good question.

When the speaker later misses this phrase out as their starting sentence, does it then mean that particular person has not asked a good question?

Continued

64

Validate the Question

Continued

As every question is valid, the answer is yes, it was. However, that is not how the person asking may feel.

When answering questions, you will be seen as more authentic by giving a thoughtful reply to address the point raised.

65

Staying on Course

While delivering your presentation, you may have questions asked that are outside of the area you have planned to cover in the time allocated.

Stay on track and ward off any temptation or questions that will divert you from your presentation purpose.

Politely let the person asking know their question is not connected with the subject and how you will be delighted to speak with them after the meeting.

66

Ask a Colleague

There may be times when you feel a colleague attending the meeting would be better placed to provide an answer to a question.

In these circumstances, you can invite them to take the question.

To save any potential awkwardness, you would only want to ask your colleague when convinced they would know the details requested.

67

Terminating the Session

While conducting your Q&A session, it will help to give notice when it will be concluding by saying something like: -

"I have time to take 3 more questions…".

Providing notice of when the Q&A session will end avoids mistakenly creating the impression you are trying to avoid answering a question if it is announced just after one has been asked.

Chapter 9

Using Your Voice and Body for Intent and Influence

68

Slowing the Speed

Your voice can be used to signpost a meaningful part of your speech.

When you are coming to a part of your presentation that contains a new idea, or maybe an important point for your audience to know, slightly slowing the speed at which you are speaking will show this is a noteworthy or serious sentence.

69

Speeding Up

The speed at which you are speaking can be changed to show different attitudes.

For example, your speaking rate can be increased to show your: -

> Excitement
>
> Emphasise light-heartedness
>
> Exhibit humour
>
> Signal that this is now a positive section of your speech

70

Authentic Connection

Most speakers know that they should aim to look around the room at everyone who is attending the meeting.

Their enthusiasm to look at all the meeting attendees can lead them to giving an impression of a spectator at a tennis match, with their head rapidly moving from side to side.

Taking the time to look naturally at the people sitting around the room is how to make an authentic connection with them.

71

Looking to Include Everyone

Focusing and making eye contact with only certain parts of the meeting room is something that can happen at times.

Speakers may look just to one side of the room or only at those seated in the first few rows.

The people sitting in all the other parts of the room will soon notice how the speaker is not looking at them and start to feel left out.

If they feel left out, they will check out from the speech.

72

Helping Hands

The importance of your hands in helping to convey the message of your speech can best be described by considering them to be the 'voice box' of body language.

The shapes, gestures and movements made will do more to communicate the importance, idea or thought you are sharing than any other part of the body.

Use your hands to make gestures that are positive and authentic to help your audience with their understanding of your speech purpose and message.

73

Sending Signals and Signs

The gestures made by a speaker can also send signals and signs that they are feeling nervous, unsure of their speech or the proposal they are presenting.

Some of the familiar gestures nervous speakers make include: -

>   Playing with their hair
>   Adjusting their glasses
>   Stroking their arm
>   Fiddling with rings or other jewellery

Continued

73

Sending Signals and Signs

Continued

Making any of these gestures is perfectly fine and will go unnoticed by the audience when made occasionally.

It is when the gestures repeatedly occur or in rapid succession that they can become distracting to everyone watching.

Continued

73

Sending Signals and Signs

Continued

Drop your hands to the sides if you should ever find yourself making the same gesture regularly or fiddling with your jewellery.

Having your hands hanging relaxed at your side is a neutral position from where you can quickly move them to make purposeful gestures.

74

What Looks Will Reveal

The meeting audience will still be observing your confidence and professionalism as you walk from the speaking area and back to your seat to sit down.

Any looks of relief, disappointment or overconfidence in those first few seconds at your seat will be noticed.

Maintain your professionalism so the audience will retain their respect for you.

Chapter 10

Recording and Reviewing

75

Filming Assistance

Many meeting and conference rooms have built-in cameras that can be used to record presentations.

The organisation's IT team may be able to organise for your presentation to be recorded and a copy to be supplied to you.

Contact them in advance of the meeting to ask if they are able to assist.

76

Repetitive and Redundant

What little gestures do you make when speaking in public that may become a distraction for the people listening to you?

Purposeful gestures and movements add to the interest and impact of your speech.

Gestures that are repetitive and unnecessary can divert attention from your words.

Watching the recording of your speech will show you any that you make, so you are able to enhance your skills.

77

Starting Similarities

While watching the recording of your speech, did you notice any of your sentences that you started with similar words?

A few of the favourite words that you will often hear other speakers using to begin their sentences are 'so', 'ok', or 'right'.

The recording of your speech will highlight any words that you may use so that you can now consider replacing them ready for your next presentation.

Chapter 11

Planning for Success

78

Planning Your Preparations

Will anyone be joining the meeting at which you are speaking via video or phone line conference call?

Ask the meeting organiser in advance as this information will help with your pre-meeting preparations.

79

Contingency Planning

Do you require access to the internet during your presentation?

Take time to ask in advance if a connection will be available as a username and password may be needed when visiting other organisations.

If the information from the internet is crucial to your presentation, download the video or take screenshots as a backup solution before the meeting.

80

Affirming Access

When you require access to the internet or company intranet for your presentation, plan to arrive at the meeting room being used early.

Open your laptop to check there is a connection to the office Wi-Fi.

Look to see that all the files and sites needed for your presentation are accessible.

81

An Outfit to Fit In

Wearing a formal suit will not always be required when speaking in public.

It all very much depends on the occasion for the presentation, the industry, who you are going to be addressing and where.

When speaking outside of your usual office environment, find out in advance what everyone will be wearing and then wear an outfit that is slightly more formal.

82

Lubricating a Symptom of Stress

One of the symptoms of public speaking stress we can experience is our throat becoming dry while delivering a presentation.

A dry throat will contribute to making delivering your presentation feel more miserable than it should ever need to be.

To help with a dry throat, arrange to have some water available in the speaking area.

Continued

82

Lubricating a Symptom of Stress

Continued

At internal company meetings, take a bottle or cup of water with you to the room, having it in place ready for your speech.

It is better for your voice to have the water at room temperature rather than chilled.

83

Taking the Time

When delivering a presentation outside of your normal business environment, you may be formally introduced to the meeting attendees.

A busy schedule can create a temptation to ask someone else to come up with something to say when they are the person introducing you.

This creates a risk of your credibility to be speaking being dented rather than boosted.

Continued

83

Taking the Time

Continued

A risk you cannot afford to take.

The person introducing you may consider the stories they tell are amusing, the jokes funny, but if they are inappropriate or fall flat, you are the one having to repair your damaged credibility.

Taking the time to create an introduction as detailed in the previous tip will ensure you start your speech on a positive note.

Public Speaking Strategies

Chapter 12

Arriving in the Room

84

Clearing the Way

The seating at larger meetings will usually be laid out in straight rows known as theatre style.

This layout looks neat and is appropriate for most meetings.

The seating arrangement may not always give those attending a clear view of the speaking area.

Before people arrive, look to see if the seating needs to be rearranged or odd chairs removed to ensure that everybody attending can see both you and your slides.

85

See and Hear

Have you added video to your slide presentation?

When your presentation has embedded video, take some time to click through your slides to see that each of the videos play as planned.

While the video is playing, move to the back and sides of the room to check the sound will clearly be heard by everyone who is attending the meeting.

86

Can You Hear Me?

Will everyone attending the meeting be able to clearly hear you delivering the speech, especially the people sitting at the back?

It is easy to check the volume you will need to speak at with the assistance of a colleague.

Before the audience arrives, ask a colleague to sit at the back while you deliver the opening few lines of your speech to see if they are able to clearly hear you.

87

Sensing the Space

In advance of delivering your speech, spend a few moments walking around the speaking area.

You will gain a sense of the space available to you while delivering your speech.

Notice if there are any trip hazards or squeaky parts of the floor that are best avoided to ensure your success.

88

High Lighting Your Speech

In large auditoriums, the lighting can sometimes be set too low so that the room falls into almost darkness.

When the lighting level is set this low, your audience will be less energetic and even tempted to close their eyes.

Maintain a high lighting level to retain high energy and engagement from the meeting attendees in your presentation.

89

Sprucing up the Suit

While standing in front of everyone attending the meeting to deliver your prepared presentation, you will naturally want to look your very best.

Take a few minutes to check yourself in a mirror before the meeting starts.

Check to see that your shirt collars are tucked in, the tie is straight, your makeup looks right, etc.

90

Stand and Stretch

If you are sitting in a large room or auditorium, a few moments before you are due to speak, walk to the back of the room.

Here you will be able to stand and stretch discreetly, helping to relieve any nervous tension.

The best place to sit is near the back of the room so it will not be too noticeable when you stand up to move.

91

Settling into Your Speech

Know off by heart the first couple of sentences that start your speech.

Any feelings of nervousness will be at their peak when you first arrive at the front of the room and move to the speaking area.

Knowing how to start your speech will help to settle you in and grow your confidence as you flawlessly deliver your opening sentences.

92

Walking Straight

When it is time to start your presentation, make your way to the speaking area, walking at a steady, purposeful pace.

If you keep your head up, shoulders straight and arms relaxed at your sides as you walk, it will externally portray that you are confident and help you to feel it.

93

Slanted Stance

A stance some speakers take while delivering their speech is to stand with their weight more on one leg, so the hips are at an angle.

This position looks and projects a casual attitude, with a risk that it can be perceived as disinterested in the subject or even the person asking you a question.

Standing straight, with your arms relaxed at your side and ready to move, is the optimal position to adopt when speaking in public.

94

Who's Listening?

Your audience may be looking at you, but have they lost interest and are no longer listening or paying attention?

Some of the signs you will see to indicate the loss of interest include: -

- Locked stare
- Their eyes fixed on the ceiling or floor
- Being focused on their phones
- Continuous whispering to colleagues
- Doodling on their notepad

95

Sensible Suggestions

If you see any of the signs from the previous tip to indicate an audience may be losing interest in your speech, do something, anything, except continuing.

Ignoring the signs can leave everyone feeling they received little value from your speech.

Practical suggestions of what to do in these situations are contained within this book and include: -

Continued

95

Sensible Suggestions

Continued

    Asking them a question

    Getting people to share something with the person next to them

    Taking a break

Creating a break in the presentation with these activities will help to ensure the attendees are able to refocus their attention on the content you are sharing with them.

96

Speaking Out Against

There may at times be different or even opposing points of view on the proposal you are presenting to the meeting.

While individually addressing these views and without being in any way disrespectful to anyone holding them, show why you are recommending the ideas in your proposal.

Showing your belief, confidence and certainty will help to convince your audience why they should be adopted.

97

Focus on Serving

While delivering presentations, you may be faced with various situations that can prove a distraction for your audience. These can include: -

- People arriving late
- People leaving early
- People whispering
- Phones ringing
- Noises coming from outside the room

Continued

97

Focus on Serving

Continued

Allowing these situations to become a distraction for you, means they will also become a distraction for everyone attending the meeting.

Maintaining your focus on serving your audience, will help ensure their attention remains on you.

98

Slow and Steady

So…do you …. erm… have the tendency to …err… scatter your speeches with filler words?

A way to help you to reduce any words and sounds like these is to speak slightly slower than your normal pace.

Speaking at a slower, steady pace will provide time for you to recall what it is you would like to say, removing the need to add any filler words or sounds.

99

Seeking Support

Ask a supportive colleague who will be attending the meeting at which you are speaking if they would make a note of any repetitive or filler words you use while delivering your speech.

These are words like so, he, she, er, um, and uh. These are the words that with repeated use, will rob your speech of power and can create a distraction for the listeners.

When you know if and when these words have been used, you will be able to work on removing them from all your future speeches.

100

Seeking the Laughter Peak

When you share a humorous story in your speech, the audience will naturally laugh along with you.

While they are laughing, pause speaking until the laughter starts to die down before carrying on with your speech.

When a speaker continues talking while everyone is still laughing, the audience will need to stop before they are ready just to hear them.

When this happens time and again, the audience will be far less likely to laugh at the next humorous story.

101

Question Yourself

On reaching the final segment of your speech, you may find you are ahead of the planned schedule.

Having this additional time provides the opportunity to ask yourself a question if you feel it is appropriate to the meeting.

Asking your own question can be achieved by saying something like "At Thursday's meeting, a question asked was…".

101 Top Secret
Public Speaking Strategies

*Speak with Confidence
Get Success!*

Andy O'Sullivan

Public Speaking Strategies

ABOUT ANDY O'SULLIVAN

How to achieve success in the business world

In his books, workshops and seminars, Andy teaches professionals how to dramatically increase their rise up the corporate career ladder and grow their business by creating and presenting presentations that inspire, impress and ensure they are the obvious choice.

Andy enjoyed a successful corporate career that saw him working for many of the leading financial institutions and international banks.

It was while working in the corporate world that Andy recognised the need to develop his own public speaking and presentation skills.

A long and, at times, painful journey that led him to develop the renowned Corporate Confidence System™.

The Corporate Confidence System™ utilises all of Andy's knowledge and extensive experience from the real world, so professionals are now able to swiftly create speeches that connect with clients, colleagues and even the CEO.

The incredible success of the Corporate Confidence System™ and constant demand by entrepreneurs and startup founders for Andy to share his extensive experience with them, led to the development of the now acclaimed Startup Success System™.

About Andy O'Sullivan

A system that ensures entrepreneurs and startup founders are able to create pitches that will impress their important investors and buyers, winning them that crucial investment or order.

The commitment Andy has continually shown in helping people to learn effective public speaking and presentation skills has been recognised by all the international awards and accolades he has received.

Andy is the founder of the Academy of Public Speakers, a leading provider of public speaking and presentation skills training.

You can contact Andy directly at: -

Andy@academyofpublicspeakers.com
www.academyofpublicspeakers.com
LinkedIn: - http://andy.chat/linkedin
Twitter: - http://andy.chat/Twitter
Facebook: - http://andy.chat/facebook
Books: - http://andy.chat/books

Acknowledgments

I will never be able to express enough thanks to my Mum for her never-ending love and support. Standing by me and always being there throughout the bad times as well as the good.

To my sister Maureen for her love, patience and fantastic assistance with this book.

To my sister Teresa for those early lessons in English.

To my brother Peter for being my willing and original chauffeur.

Thanks to Hien Vo for always finding time for me, his valued support, ongoing encouragement and cherished friendship.

To Tanvir Arafat for being a constant source of inspiration and enthusiasm. His continual energy and encouragement helping to propel me ever forwards.

Thanks to Keny Castro-Moreno for his willing and awesome support he provided with my recent books.

To Naynesh Patel for always being there and willing to give me a helping hand whenever I asked and even when I didn't.

Thanks to Rob Hemsley for his ardent assistance with the PR machine he very kindly created and managed.

Thanks to Shyam Gupta for seeing the potential in me and giving up his time to help at my first series of events.

Acknowledgments

Thanks to Michael for working so hard to give us all that he possibly could.

To Ralph C. Smedley without whom my journey of self-development and growth would have been so much longer and harder.

A final word of gratitude to all those who have guided and supported me during my long and at times painful journey.

Public Speaking Strategies

References

Mail Online (2018). Scientists reveal the harder you chew gum, the greater the relief. [online] Available at: http://www.dailymail.co.uk/health/article-3241135/Gum-keeps-Jose-ball-Scientists-reveal-harder-chew-greater-relief.html. Web. 3 Feb. 2018

Rodionova, Zlata. "The 12 Words To Say In An Interview That Can Land (Or Lose) You The Job". The Independent. N.p., 2016. Web. 1 Apr. 2016.

"Serial Position Effect ". Indiana.edu. N.p., 2016. Web. 1 Apr. 2016.

"Presentation - Definition Of Presentation In English From The Oxford Dictionary". Oxforddictionaries.com. N.p., 2016. Web. 1 Apr. 2016.

"Pitch - Definition Of Pitch In English From The Oxford Dictionary". Oxforddictionaries.com. N.p., 2016. Web. 1 Apr. 2016.

"7 Shocking Health Statistics". Realbuzz 4. N.p., 2012. Web. 1 Apr. 2016.

Bibliography

Avery, Matt. Successful Public Speaking In A Week. London: Teach Yourself, 2013. Print.

Beebe, Steven, and Beebe, Susan. Public Speaking, An Audience-Centered Approach. Mass.: Pearson, 2013. Print

Eldin, Peter et al. Speechmakers' Bible. London: Cassell Illustrated, 2006. Print.

Fripp, Patricia and LaCroix. Create Your Keynote By Next Week. USA: DVD.

Godefroy, Christian H, Stephanie Barrat-Godefroy, and Christian Godefroy. Confident Public Speaking. London: Piatkus, 1998. Print.

Jeffreys, Michael. Success Secrets Of The Motivational Superstars. Rocklin, CA: Prima Pub., 1996. Print.

Ledden, Emma. The Presentation Book. Harlow: Pearson, 2013. Print.

Linver, Sandy, and Jim Mengert. Speak And Get Results. New York: Simon & Schuster, 1994. Print.

Lucas, Stephen. The Art Of Public Speaking. Boston: McGraw-Hill Higher Education, 2009. Print.

Mueck, Florian. The Seven Minute Star. [North Charleston, S.C.]: [Createspace], 2010. Print.

Valentine, Craig, and Mitch Meyerson. World Class Speaking In Action. New York: Morgan James, 2015 Print.

Weissman, Jerry, and Jerry Weissman. Successful Presentation Strategies. Upper Saddle, New Jersey: FT Press, 2013. Print.

Yazbeck, Joe. No Fear Speaking. Odessa, FL: Paradies Publishing Co., 2014. Print.

www.ingramcontent.com/pod-product-compliance
Lightning Source LLC
Chambersburg PA
CBHW052252220526
45471CB00001B/304